ANNIE LAPIN

THE ART OF HEADS AND HANDS

MILES
McENERY
GALLERY

520 West 21st Street
New York NY 10011

tel +1 212 445 0051
www.milesmcenery.com

525 West 22nd Street
New York NY 10011

ANNIE LAPIN: THE ARCHAEOLOGY OF MEANING

By Julia Friedman

Hands are almost living beings.[1]
—Henri Focillon

Annie Lapin's paintings are old souls. They are developed, unhurried, protean, but they resist interpretation, permitting only provisional glimpses into what the mind already knows. Despite the multitude of allusions packed into them, even recognizable references to a variety of artistic styles—Rococo, Surrealism, Color Field Abstraction—function more like epistemological teasers, rather than keys to the works' semantic ambiguity. Structurally, too, there is not much to grasp onto: the compositional push/pull of the paintings adds a strong temporal quality, complicating legibility at a glance. Yet, none come across as overworked meta-commentaries on the art historical canon, or gratuitous displays of artistic dexterity.

Lapin's paintings test the viewer's ability to withstand what she calls "the chaos of modern perceptual experience," transforming "the random meanderings of a mind" into a coherent narrative. Her working method is characterized by her insistence on combining spontaneity and deliberation. She refuses to harness her imagery, relying on the unpredictability of the pouring process in the initial stages of her painting. This step is indispensible for enabling the next, free association, which in turn leads to a series of intuitive choices. From this point on, the process moves laterally between creating imagery and interpreting it, until the forms themselves distill the meaning of the work. Lapin shuns narratives imposed onto paintings. Instead, she takes the arduous path of unearthing the painting's intrinsic meaning—not unlike an archaeologist who toils to recognize, reveal, and reconfigure objects concealed in the ruins of the past. Only Lapin's archaeology is the archaeology of meaning.

1. Henri Focillon, *The Life of Forms in Art*, trans. Charles Beecher Hogan and George Kubler, New Haven: Yale University Press, 1942. All of the Focillon quotations in this essay are from this work.

It may not be a coincidence that Lapin began as an archaeology major at Yale University (where she did her undergraduate work) before switching to art and subsequently pursuing post-bac-calaureate studies at the Art Institute of Chicago. She earned an MFA from the University of California, Los Angeles in 2007. Lapin has had a number of solo exhibitions in Los Angeles (Honor Fraser Gallery), London (Josh Lilley Gallery), Naples (Annarumma Gallery), and Mexico City (Yautepec Gallery), as well as at the Weatherspoon Art Museum in Greensboro, North Carolina, and the Museum of Contemporary Art Santa Barbara, in Santa Barbara, California.

The current body of work, entitled *The Art of Heads and Hands*, continues the stylistic trajectory of her most recent exhibition, *Watchers and Winks*, held in late 2016 at the Honor Fraser Gallery. Only now, the perceptual chaos is intensified in direct proportion to the sociopolitical upheavals that have taken place since the show opened on November 5, 2016. While Lapin's work is too subtle to tackle politics head-on, the paintings in *The Art of Heads and Hands* seek certainty through clashing figurative and abstract elements. Notwithstanding the political climate in the aftermath of the 2016 election, and the subsequent soul-searching among the art crowd, Lapin resists giving up her supple approach to the search of meaning in favor of declarative statements. Rejecting the potentially soothing imposition of constructed meaning, she perseveres in follow-ing all the necessary "iterations of mental responses" until "the forms call" to her.

If this insistence on the sentient character and the agency of form sounds familiar, it is because Lapin's conviction that form itself can generate meaning has an earlier precedent in the art his-torical canon. In an age dominated by the deterministic doctrines of Alois Riegl, Heinrich Wölfflin, and Erwin Panofsky, all based, to a degree, on the Hegelian notion of history's progressive unfold-ing, a French scholar, Henri Focillon (1881–1943), put forth a different theory that presented form as a living entity and subject to disruptions by historical and social forces. Focillon, who wrote his doctoral dissertation (1918) on the maverick of spatial play, engraver Giovanni Battista Piranesi, was an art historian of wide-ranging interests. He wrote on a variety of subjects in Western and non-Western art, including Cellini (1911), Hokusai (1914), Buddhist art (1921), nineteenth century painting (1927) and the art of the Middle Ages (1933, 1938, 1943). His unorthodox ideas on form, formulated in a short book, *Vie des formes*, were originally published in 1934. *The Life of Forms in Art*, as it became known in English, was in part Focillon's response to political events in Germany—his scholarly and civic contribution to the defense of humanistic ideals. Following Hitler's rise to power, Focillon, then the chairman of aesthetics and history of art at Collège de France, was invited to join Yale University (Lapin's alma mater) as a visiting faculty member. After France was occupied in 1939, Focillon made the United States his home. He died in New Haven on March 3, 1943.

Focillon believed that forms come into being from the visual world of multiple temporalities, where each temporality is superimposed onto other temporalities. Thus, the history of art is not a string of successive periods and styles, but an intricate cultural layering that allows for simultaneity within duration. His view of history as nonlinear, as "the superimposition of very widely spaced present moments" was based on the assumption that "various modes of action are contemporaneous, that is, seized upon at the same moment." The cross-section of breaks and fissures in Lapin's paintings is a perfect embodiment for Focillon's geological metaphor of art history not as a progression, but as a "layering of geological strata, in which certain abrupt fault lines, certain canyons, reveal at a single glance the existence of simultaneity within duration." According to Focillon, if we were to choose an arbitrary point in a chronological continuum, "politics, economics and art [would] not occupy identical positions on their respective graphs, and the line joining them at any one given moment [would be] more often than not a very irregular and sinuous one." While such an understanding of history is hardly shocking within the context of postmodern relativism, in the 1930s Focillon's ideas were conspicuously at odds with the prevailing binary framework and understanding of time.

Focillon saw the works of art, and the forms within them, as culture-transcendent, "immersed in the whirlpool of time" and belonging to eternity. For him, works of art are at once "specific, local, individual," a "metaphor of the entire universe," and "a bright token of universality," much as for Lapin they are "fragments of the real landscape that mesh with art historical landscapes and bits of [her] own interior landscape." One of Focillon's basic arguments against the homogeneous constraints of iconographical analysis, in which forms have predetermined and fixed meanings, is that the same images can be perceived differently within varied temporal and cultural contexts. Sensitivity to the diversity of perceptions is second nature to Lapin. As a child, she was exposed to vastly different cultural environments, ranging from Washington D.C., to a small town in the Kentucky Bible Belt, to Tokyo, where she attended high school. For Lapin, the notion that a stain, a symbol or even a color can register differently, depending on the viewers' geographical or cultural background, is central in organizing her painting to enable interaction at the unconscious level, beyond the faculties of language.

Language is an important category for Lapin, as it was for Focillon. In his view, "human consciousness is in perpetual pursuit of a language and a style," so "to assume consciousness is at once to assume form." This is key to Lapin's practice. Her veneration of organically produced meaning strongly suggests that she would support Focillon's assertion: "The chief characteristic of the mind is to be constantly describing itself. The mind is a design that is in a state of ceaseless flux, of ceaseless weaving and then unweaving, and its activity, in this sense, is an artistic activity." Lapin's search for meaning reverberates with Focillon's belief in that forms always tend towards realization, and that "form, guided by the play and interplay of metamorphoses, [will] go forever forward, by its own necessity, towards its own liberty." The artist's task, then, is to aid in the liberation of form.

Lapin's technique, which is both varying and complex, is a perfect example of what Focillon describes as "the analysis ... of the preliminary ideas, the sketches, the rough drafts that precede the finished statue or painting." Her concurrent visual analysis provides a record not just of "a jumbled topography of successive states of consciousness," but also of "the very technique of the life of forms itself, its own biological development." For Lapin, this is a stage in "a process of spinning a narrative."

Lapin's understanding of the way meaning coagulates within the works of art, her awareness of the shifting, evolving nature of meaning and the continuous morphing of painterly form, her reluctance to pin down the space, her reliance on a broad range of media and representational styles (construction, abstraction, figuration) index her serendipitous affinity with Focillon's ideas. Take, for example, Lapin's thesis that the meaning of her painting is the end point of a long process prompted by a physical stimulus, and shaped through a series of mental and psychic responses to the images on the canvas. Focillon's model of form as a vessel for meaning presumes that old meanings are continuously broken down, while new ones attach themselves to form. In Focillon's view, form possesses its own intrinsic meaning. He warns against the tendency to see form as a mere signifier of what he calls "a wholly deliberate content," pointing out the danger of form being "tortured to fit a meaning." Lapin is equally vigilant not to impose meaning onto her paintings, allowing the meaning to distill itself through forms.

Natural evolution of forms is a central concept for Focillon. For all their autonomous quality, forms have anthropological connections both on the part of their creator, the artist, and on the part of their recipient, the viewer: "They mingle with life, whence they come; they translate into space certain movements of the mind." Focillon brings up this form/life/mind trifecta time and again, referring to form as "the translation of a free and exalted dream," which "prolongs and diffuses itself throughout our dreams and fancies." His notion of form as a realm "which is neither that of physical extent nor that of pure thought" echoes Lapin's reliance on a combination of physical gestures and intuition in her work.

The paintings in the exhibition illustrate the idea of the continuous metamorphosis of forms, which leads to unremitting shifts in meaning. Thus, *California* contains "Western" tropes (a sunset, a horse, perhaps the shoreline of a stream in the wilderness), alongside an Édouard Manet-like landscape that reappears in *The Clamor to Get Inside and Outside*. As Focillon stated, "nature as well as life creates forms," and Lapin's use of nature, especially her inclusion of the realistically rendered sky and clouds throughout *The Art of Heads and Hands* series suggests just that. For Focillon, "life is form, and form is the modality of life," so "the relationships that bind forms together in nature cannot be pure chance." For him, "What we call 'natural life' is in effect a relationship between forms." Lapin's skillfully rendered combinations of mimetic landscape fragments and superimposed geometric grids in *The Light Became Thick* is one good example.

The affinities do not stop here. Lapin's *Three Versions Play* could serve as an illustration for Focillon's theory of forms in the realm of space, as it clearly "treats space according to its own needs, defines space, and even creates such space as may be necessary to it." A subtle appending of fibers to the surface of the painting adds complicated spatial play, as do the oddly shaped portions of stretcher bars. Lapin's sophisticated use of physical variations and dimensionality correlates to Focillon's theory of spaces as limits vs. spaces as environments.

Focillon's classification of the art workspace into ornamental, scenic, or cartographic, and his insistence that the space of the art is always connected to the space of the real world, is handy for analyzing one of the most complex paintings in the show *The Herd, The Heard, The Hoard*—a double-paneled palimpsest of abstraction, figuration, and illusionistic overlays. Similarly on point is his comment: "By means of *trompe-l'oeil*, perspective completely demolishes architecture and shatters its ceilings with one explosive apotheosis after another. [It] wipes out the boundaries of stage scenery by creating a false infinity and an illusory vastness." This comment is nothing short of an *avant la lettre* description of *Stop Calling*, where a Rococo-inspired landscape morphs into a Surrealist-looking human limb sunk into the canvas by an angled lip of the painting. Focillon would probably credit this sort of spatial complexity to "metamorphoses exploiting deductions to the last possible limits ... tirelessly evoking all manner of new relations between form and space."

In the final chapter of *The Life of Forms in Art*, entitled "In Praise of Hands," Focillon tells a story of the great Japanese master Hokusai, who is said to have attempted a painting without using his hands as artists conventionally do. Hokusai started his process by pouring paint, creating, to the audience's delight, a recognizable mimetic representation of a local stream through a "concord between accident, study and dexterity." Lapin's working method, which also originates with pouring (charcoal and water over static-like yellow paint), aims at a similar combination of accident, study, and dexterity. Only then, does she go through the steps of looking, choosing and making painterly marks.

As the title of her current exhibition, *The Art of Heads and Hands,* suggests, hands have symbolic significance for Lapin as well. The title, taken from one of the paintings in the show, highlights the philosophical bifurcation she sees in the traditional manuals on figurative painting. At once, pedestrian instruction tools and semi-mystical manifestations of collective consciousness, these manuals function as a perfect point of departure for further exploration in search of what Focillon labels "curious possibilities."

As Lapin juxtaposes figuration and abstraction, flatness and recession, clarity and haziness, she reinforces the idea that possibilities are chances, and chances are randomness, making her paintings the site of exploration. The nimble spatial interplay of clefts and slippage in *The Art of Heads and Hands* is Lapin's way of conjuring up the hidden "ghost forms of figures and archaeological decay," her way of unearthing meaning. ∎

Dr. Julia Friedman is an independent art historian, curator and critic. She is a regular contributor to *Artforum, The New Criterion,* and *HuffPost.* In 2011, Northwestern University Press published her monograph *Beyond Symbolism and Surrealism: Alexei Remizov's Synthetic Art.* Her most recent book project was based on the digital writings of Dave Hickey.

iheroic

We Beam Passed

The Clamor to Get Inside and Outside

Whereview II

Art of Heads and Hands

Stop Calling

Martinique the Gentlefool

Choral Remarks

Defenestration

Three Versions Play

Turf Tiff

California

To Sit and Think

The Herd, The Heard, The Hoard

The Light Became Thick

Eachother

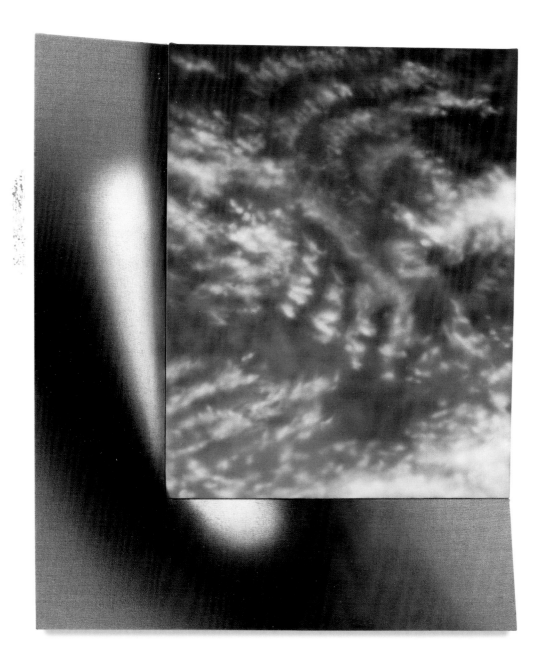

Plate List

page 11

iheroic, 2018
Vinyl paint, charcoal, acrylic and
urethane on linen
30 x 26 x 3 inches
76.2 x 66 x 7.6 cm

page 13

We Beam Passed, 2018
Vinyl paint, charcoal, acrylic and
urethane on linen
30 x 26 x 3 inches
76.2 x 66 x 7.6 cm

page 15

The Clamor to Get Inside and Outside, 2018
Oil, vinyl paint, acrylic, charcoal and
mica on linen
72 x 96 inches
182.9 x 243.8 cm

page 17

Whereview II, 2018
Vinyl paint, mica, charcoal, acrylic and
urethane on linen
30 x 26 x 3 inches
76.2 x 66 x 7.6 cm

page 19

Art of Heads and Hands, 2018
Oil, oil stick, vinyl paint, acrylic and
charcoal on linen
72 x 96 inches
182.9 x 243.8 cm

page 21

Stop Calling, 2018
Oil, acrylic, charcoal and
vinyl paint on linen
30 x 26 x 3 inches
76.2 x 66 x 7.6 cm

page 23

Martinique the Gentlefool, 2018
Oil, vinyl paint, acrylic, nylon flocking and
charcoal on linen
72 x 96 inches
182.9 x 243.8 cm

page 25

Choral Remarks, 2018
Charcoal, acrylic and
vinyl paint on linen
30 x 26 x 3 inches
76.2 x 66 x 7.6 cm

ANNIE LAPIN

Born in Washington, D.C., in 1978
Lives and works in Los Angeles, CA

EDUCATION

2007
MFA, University of California, Los Angeles, CA

2004
Post-Baccalaureate Certificate, School of the Art Institute of Chicago,
    Chicago, IL

2001
BA, Yale University, New Haven, CT

SOLO EXHIBITIONS

2018
 "The Art of Heads and Hands," Miles McEnery Gallery, New York, NY

2016
"Watchers and Winks," Honor Fraser Gallery, Los Angeles, CA
"How to Bury Your Stuff," Josh Lilley Gallery, London, United Kingdom

2014
"Various Peep Shows," Honor Fraser Gallery, Los Angeles, CA
"See?," Annarumma Gallery, Naples, Italy

2013
"Annie Lapin: Falk Visiting Artist," Weatherspoon Art Museum,
    Greensboro, NC
"Amnesiacs," Josh Lilley Gallery, London, United Kingdom

2012
"Find Finding ing," Yautepec Gallery, Mexico City, Mexico
"History=ing," Museum of Contemporary Art, Santa Barbara, CA

2011
"Ideal Idyl Idol," Annarumma Gallery, Naples, Italy
"The Pure Space Animate," Honor Fraser Gallery, Los Angeles, CA

2009
"Parallel Deliria Iteration," Pasadena Museum of California Art,
    Pasadena, CA

2008
"Parallel Deliria," Grand Arts, Kansas City, MO
"Gruppology," Angles Gallery, Santa Monica, CA

2000
"Paintings and Prints," Davenport Studio 54, New Haven, CT

GROUP EXHIBITIONS

2018
"Belief in Giants," Miles McEnery Gallery, New York, NY

2017
"The Ecstasy of Mary Shelley," Los Angeles Contemporary Exhibitions,
    Los Angeles, CA

2016
"Her Crowd: New Art by Women from Our Neighbors' Private
    Collections," Bruce Museum, Greenwich, CT

2015
"Tribal Tats," Arturo Bandini, Los Angeles, CA
"Angels with Dirty Faces," Hilger Contemporary, Vienna, Austria
"Lost in a Sea of Red," The Pit, Los Angeles, CA
"Sincerely Yours," Torrance Art Museum, Torrance, CA

2014
"The Go-Between," Museo di Capodimonte, Naples, Italy
"Dee Ferris, Barnaby Furnas, Annie Lapin," Sargent's Daughters, New
    York, NY

2013
"B.A.T. (Bon à Tirer/Good to Go)," Offramp Gallery, Pasadena, CA
"Annie Lapin, John Lehr, Alon Levin, Philip Vanderhyden," Andrew
    Rafacz Gallery, Chicago, IL
"Fanatic," PØST, Los Angeles, CA
"Raw Material," Yautepec Gallery, Mexico City, Mexico

2012
"Stone Gravy" (curated by David Pagel), Ameringer | McEnery | Yohe, New York, NY
"Chasm of the Supernova" (curated by Adam Miller), Center for the Arts Eagle Rock, Los Angeles, CA

2011
"Sentimental Education," Gavlak Gallery, Palm Beach, FL
"Incredulous Zealots: 4 Painterly Interrogations from LA," Josh Lilley Gallery, London, United Kingdom
"La Californie," The Museum of Public Fiction, Los Angeles, CA
"Baker's Dozen III," Torrance Art Museum, Torrance, CA
"Unfinished Paintings" (curated by Kristin Calabrese and Joshua Aster), Los Angeles Contemporary Exhibitions, Los Angeles, CA
"The Open Daybook Exhibition," Los Angeles Contemporary Exhibitions, Los Angeles, CA
"Plentitude," Barbara Davis Gallery, Houston, TX
"Five from L.A.," Galerie Lelong, New York, NY

2010
"Larval Stages," Latned Atsär Studio, Los Angeles, CA
"Living with Art: Collecting Contemporary in Metro New York," Neuberger Museum of Art, Purchase, NY
"I'll Let You Be in My Dreams if I Can Be in Yours," Fredericks & Freiser Gallery, New York, NY

2009
"Rogue Wave '09," L.A. Louver, Venice, CA
"Bitch Is the New Black," Honor Fraser Gallery, Los Angeles, CA
"NewNow," Nerman Museum of Contemporary Art, Overland Park, KS

2008
"L.A. Now," Las Vegas Art Museum, Las Vegas, NV
"LA25 Half-Life," Los Angeles Contemporary Exhibitions, Los Angeles, CA
"The Unruly and the Humorous," Angles Gallery, Santa Monica, CA
"Probably," Inman Gallery, Houston, TX
"Some Paintings: LA Weekly Annual Biennial," Track 16 Gallery, Santa Monica, CA

2007
"Bliss," Roberts & Tilton, Los Angeles, CA
"LA 25," Skadden, Arps, Slate, Meagher & Flom, Los Angeles, CA

"GLAMFA," California State University, Long Beach, CA
"Block Party II," Daniel Weinberg Gallery, Los Angeles, CA
"Summer Stock," Angles Gallery, Los Angeles, CA
"New Wight Gallery," University of California, Los Angeles, CA

2006
"Annual Group Show," Taylor de Cordoba, Los Angeles, CA
"Henry Painter," Bronson Tropics, Los Angeles, CA

2005
"The Fall of the House...," California State Polytechnic University, Pomona, CA
"The Great Outdoors," Angles Gallery, Santa Monica, CA

2004
Graduate Exhibition, School of the Art Institute of Chicago, Chicago, IL

2001
Yale School of Art Exhibition, Yale University, New Haven, CT

2000
"Painting Pots and Prints," Studio 54, New Haven, CT
"Chautauqua Paintings," Calhoun Cabaret, New Haven, CT

PUBLIC AND ACADEMIC LECTURES

2017
Claremont Graduate University, Visiting Artist Lecture Series, Claremont, CA

2016
University of California, Irvine, Visiting Artist Lecture Series, Irvine, CA

2015
San Francisco Art Institute, Visiting Artist Lecture Series, San Francisco, CA
University of California, Davis, Visiting Artist Lecture Series, Davis, CA

2013
University of California, Santa Barbara, Artist Speaking Series, Santa Barbara, CA
Otis College of Art and Design Visiting Artist Lecture Series, Los Angeles, CA

2012

Michigan State University Department of Art, Art History, and Design, Lansing, MI

California State University, Northridge, Hans Burkhardt Speaker, Northridge, CA

University of California, Los Angeles, MFA Visiting Artist Series, Los Angeles, CA

2011

Honor Fraser Gallery, Public Conversation with Ed Schad, Los Angeles, CA

2009

College Art Association, Panel Discussion with David Pagel, Los Angeles, CA

2008

Grand Arts, Lecture and Conversation with Robert Stilling, Kansas City, MO

AWARDS AND RESIDENCIES

2013

Weatherspoon Art Museum, Falk Visiting Artist Award, Greensboro, NC

Anderson Ranch Arts Center, Snowmass Village, CO

2008

Grand Arts, Kansas City, MO

2002

Burren College of Art, Ballyvaughn, Ireland

2000

Chautauqua Institutution, Chautauqua, New York, NY

PUBLICATIONS

Ed Schad, *Annie Lapin: The Pure Space Animate*. Los Angeles: Honor Fraser Inc., 2011

David P. Earle, *The Open Day Book*. New York: Random House, 2010

COLLECTIONS

High Museum of Art, Atlanta, GA

Los Angeles County Museum of Art, Los Angeles, CA

Nerman Museum of Contemporary Art, Overland Park, KS

Orange County Museum of Art, Newport Beach, CA

Rubell Family Collection, Miami, FL

Santa Barbara Museum of Art, Santa Barbara, CA

Weatherspoon Art Museum, Greensboro, NC

Zabludowicz Collection, London, United Kingdom.

Published on the occasion of the exhibition

ANNIE LAPIN
THE ART OF HEADS AND HANDS

11 October – 10 November 2018

Miles McEnery Gallery
525 West 22nd Street
New York NY 10011

tel +1 212 445 0051
www.milesmcenery.com

Photography by
Christopher Burke Studio, New York, NY

Catalogue designed by
HHA Design, New York, NY

ISBN: 978-1-949327-00-7

Cover
California (detail), 2018

Miles McEnery Gallery would like to thank
Honor Fraser Gallery and Dr. Julia Friedman

MILES
McENERY
GALLERY